POODLES

by Martha E. H. Rustad

AMICUS HIGH INTEREST • AMICUS INK

Amicus High Interest and Amicus Ink are imprints of Amicus
P.O. Box 1329, Mankato, MN 56002
www.amicuspublishing.us

Library of Congress Cataloging-in-Publication Data
Names: Rustad, Martha E. H. (Martha Elizabeth Hillman), 1975- author.
Title: Poodles / by Martha E. H. Rustad.
Description: Mankato, Minnesota : Amicus High Interest, Amicus Ink,
  [2018] | Series: Favorite dog breeds | Audience: K to grade 3. | Includes
  bibliographical references and index.
Identifiers: LCCN 2016034043 (print) | LCCN 2016040770 (ebook) | ISBN
  9781681511290 (library binding) | ISBN 9781681521602 (pbk.) | ISBN
  9781681512198 (ebook) | ISBN 9781681512198 (eBook)
Subjects: LCSH: Poodles--Juvenile literature. | Dog breeds--Juvenile
  literature.
Classification: LCC SF429.P85 R87 2018 (print) | LCC SF429.P85 (ebook) |
  DDC 636.72/8--dc23
LC record available at https://lccn.loc.gov/2016034043

Photo Credits: Lim Tiaw Leong/Shutterstock cover; Ivan Vdovin/Alamy
Stock Photo 5; P Reinagle in Taplin's Sportsman's Cabinet/Mary Evans
Picture Library 6-7; Jagodka/Shutterstock 2, 9, 14-15; Andrew Burton/
Getty Images 10-11; s5iztok/istock 12-13; zakaz/Alamy Stock Photo
17; Lise Goulet/Dreamstime.com 18; Leren Lu/Getty 21; Eric Isselee/
Shutterstock 22

Editor: Wendy Dieker
Designer: Tracy Myers
Photo Researcher: Holly Young

TABLE OF CONTENTS

LEARNING TRICKS

A dog stands up on her two back legs. She walks. The crowd cheers. Her owner gives her a treat. Poodles are smart pets. They can be **trained** to do lots of tricks.

WATER DOG

The poodle breed started in Germany. The old German word *pudel* meant "to splash." The first poodles fetched birds in water for hunters. Poodles today still like to swim.

Furry Fact
Poodles are called *caniche* in France. That means "duck dog."

THREE SIZES

Poodles can be three sizes.

Standard poodles are large dogs.

Miniature poodles are medium

sized. Toy poodles are small dogs.

They all look alike.

NO SHEDDING

The poodle breed sheds very little. Their hair grows and grows. Groomers cut the hair. Poodles in dog shows have fancy haircuts.

JUMPING

Poodles can jump high. Some poodles train for **agility courses**. They jump through hoops. They leap over **hurdles**.

POODLE PUPPIES

Three to six puppies are born in each poodle **litter**. Standard pups are larger than miniature pups. Toy pups are smallest. Puppy fur colors can change as they grow.

Furry Fact

A poodle's fur is usually one of ten solid colors. Some poodles have two colors.

POODLE JOBS

Poodles learn quickly. These smart dogs seem to enjoy learning new things. Some poodles work as **service dogs**. Other poodles perform on stage. Poodles also work as hunting dogs.

WATCHDOGS

Poodles can be good watchdogs. They bark to alert owners of new people. These dogs like to protect their families. They like to keep their **territory** safe.

FRIENDLY PETS

Poodles do not like to be alone.

They like to play with their owners.

They are good with children.

Poodles can be great family pets.

HOW DO YOU KNOW IT'S A POODLE?

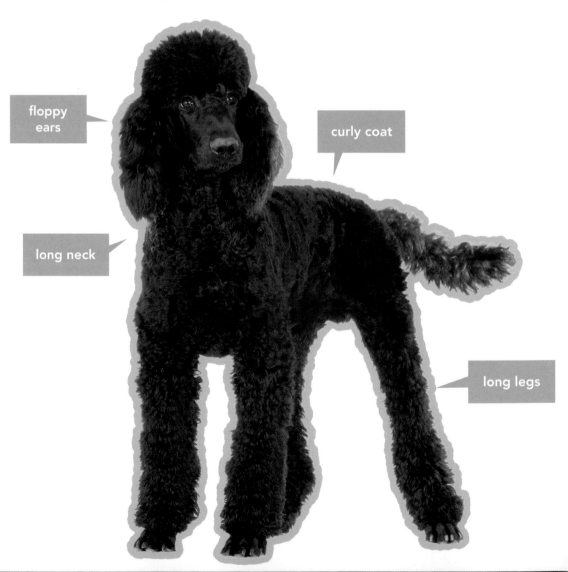

floppy ears

curly coat

long neck

long legs

WORDS TO KNOW

agility course – a contest where dogs run an obstacle course of ramps, tunnels, and hoops as fast as they can

hurdle – a bar to jump over

litter – a group of puppies born at the same time

service dog – a dog that is trained to help people

territory – a certain area that an animal lives in and works to protect

train – to teach an animal how to behave or how to do tricks

LEARN MORE

Books

Berry, Breanna. *Poodles*. Blastoff! Readers. Awesome Dogs. Minneapolis: Bellwether Media, 2016.

Bodden, Valerie. *Poodles*. Fetch! Mankato, Minn.: Creative Education, 2014.

Websites

American Kennel Club: Poodle
http://www.akc.org/dog-breeds/poodle/

The Poodle
http://www.loveyourdog.com/poodles.html

INDEX